KABUIKA Wants to Make New Friends

Kabuika Wants to Make New Friends

Kabuika Kamunga

Copyright © 2020 Kabuika Kamunga

Published by 1st World Publishing
P.O. Box 2211, Fairfield, Iowa 52556
tel: 641-209-5000 • fax: 866-440-5234
web: www.1stworldpublishing.com

First Edition
LCCN: 2020932622
ISBN: 978-1-4218-3659-1

All rights reserved. No part of this book may be reproduced or utilized in any form or by any means, electronic or mechanical, including photocopying or recording, or by any information storage and retrieval system, without permission in writing from the author.

This material has been written and published for educational purposes to enhance one's well-being. In regard to health issues, the information is not intended as a substitute for appropriate care and advice from health professionals, nor does it equate to the assumption of medical or any other form of liability on the part of the publisher or author. The publisher and author shall have neither liability nor responsibility to any person or entity with respect to loss, damages, or injury claimed to be caused directly or indirectly by any information in this book.

I like to wear matching African fabrics with my doll Kabedi.

"Her clothes are different."

I like to eat fried plantains with mayonnaise and ketchup.

I like to have my hair braided with threads in the fashion of my culture.

Lundi	Banane plantain	Makuenda Makanga
Mardi	Frites	Bilunga bikanga
Mercredi	Makelele	Mienza Mikanga
Jeudi	Poulet grillé	Tshibemba tshikanga
Vendredi	Beignets	Bitumbula bikanga
Samedi	Poisson grillé	Bikela bikanga
Dimanche	Viande de chèvre grillée	Munyinyi wa mbuji mukanga

"Kabuika is from the Congo. For Show and Tell today, she will tell us about her family," says my teacher.

I brought my doll Kabedi. Kabedi is my memory doll. She helps me remember my whole family tree. Each patch on her clothes represents an ancestor on my tree, you see!

This patch is for my Mom, Malu. She fixes my hair every week. I love her very much.
This patch is for my Dad, Kamunga. He's a doctor.

My Dad is the first pediatrician of the Congo. We came to the US so that he can do research.

This patch is for my grandpa Kabeya. I miss him. He
This patch is for my ancestor Muadi.

The name of our village is Bena Muadi, because we are descendants of Muadi.

And these patches here are

for my ancestors Kalonji and his wife Kabedi.

Kalonji had more than 12 children. An entire new tribe was born from him. Luba is my ethnic group. Bakwa kalonji is my tribe. We are the biggest tribe in Congo.

"Let's introduce ourselves to Kabuika," says my teacher.
"Hi Kabuika ! My name is Ami. I'm from North Carolina."
"I am Jim and this is my sister Nesta. We're from Minnesota."
"Hi Kabuika ! I am Jennifer from Indiana."
"I'm Benjy from Chicago."

We thought you were different, but you're just like us. You have parents and grandparents. We all want to be your friends.

My new favorite food is a cheese sandwich made out of fried plantains.

my culture too. At my birthday party, fabrics. And some even changed ...

... their hairstyle.

Kabuika enjoys traveling and meeting people. She had just come out of the rainforest in Congo when she heard that her first book was published. When people ask her where she is from, Kabuika replies, "I'm from ChiCongo. I'm from Chicago and the Congo." Kabuika loves to immerse herself in different cultures. She speaks French, English, Lingala and is learning Tshiluba. This book is inspired by her life story.

Bilakov is an illustrator from Congo. He lives in Kinshasa. He loves to draw comic books and mangas. Bilakov says his name means the Peace Warrior. This is his first children's book.

"To Kanyinda Bululu Etienne Marcel
who taught me how to introduce myself the Luba way."

For fun activities about Kabuika Makes New Friends,
Visit www.kabuikakamunga.com

Other books by Kabuika Kamunga
I Used to be Afraid of Animals

www.ingramcontent.com/pod-product-compliance
Lightning Source LLC
Chambersburg PA
CBHW081331040426
42453CB00013B/2379